ARRESTED FOR DWI IN MINNESOTA?

(WHAT YOU NEED TO KNOW TO FIGHT YOUR DWI)

DISCLAIMER:

This publication is intended to be informational only. No legal advice is being given, and no attorney-client relationship is intended to be created by reading this material. If you are facing legal issues, whether criminal or civil, seek professional legal counsel to get your questions answered.

Thomas Hagen

Rosengren Kohlmeyer Law Office, Chtd.

150 Saint Andrews Ct, Suite 110

Mankato, MN 56001

www.MankatoDWI.com

(507) 625-5000

TESTIMONIAL:

"Tom saved my career! I was facing a DWI that had the potential to ruin my career. Tom put together a great case and had it dismissed! I didn't even know that was possible. I still have a my job and attribute that to Tom's hard work on my case."---- D.D

"Mr. Hagen is a great lawyer. He was always available to answer questions regarding my case and took time to explain everything to me. He always arrivedearly and prepared for court appearances. I would recommend him." --- G.A

"I am so glad that I hired Tom Hagen for my DWI. Not only did I get a good outcome for my case, but I was always able to talk to him not an answering machine. You saved me from losing my job and for that I am so very thankful"--- Former DWI Client

---

"Mr. Hagen is very understanding, compassionate and a reliable lawyer. I would highly recommend him to others." --- D.A.

Table of Contents

ATTORNEY INTRODUCTION

Thomas K. Hagen is an partner at Rosengren Kohlmeyer Law Office, Chtd. located in Mankato, Minnesota. He specializes in criminal law with a focus on Driving While Impaired (DWI) cases. His credentials include being named a "Rising Star" by Minneapolis-St. Paul Magazine. In fact, Tom was the only out-state attorney to receive this award for criminal defense in Minnesota in 2012.This award is given out to the top 2.5% of attorneys in Minnesota, under the age of 40, as selected by their peers. Tom lives in Mankato with his wife Amy and son Will.

Is A DUI Different From A DWI?

Different states have different terminology for driving while intoxicated. People commonly hear DUI or driving under the influence. Minnesota technically does not have a DUI charge. Rather, Minnesota only has a DWI (driving while intoxicated) charge. The terminology of a DWI and a DUI can be interchangeable. They are similar in nature in the fact that they both outlaw driving a motor vehicle while being intoxicated.

Normally in a DWI case, the State will charge a defendant with multiple charges of DWI. The first charge is what I call an old fashioned DWI. This is when the officer, based upon his observations and field sobriety tests, believes an individual is under the influence of alcohol. The second charge is the more common thought of DWI, which is when their blood alcohol concentration is over .08.

DWI 101 – AN OVERVIEW

In most cases, here is what happens:

- The police officer will make a stop of your vehicle.
- The police officer will notice the odor of alcohol.
- You will be asked to step out of the vehicle.
- You will be asked to perform "standardized field sobriety tests", which usually consists of a 9 step walk-and-turn test, a 30 second leg lift and the horizontal gaze nystagmus test.
- You will be given a preliminary breath testing device (PBT). This is also known as a breathalyzer, a small black box you will be asked to blow into that measures the alcohol level that is in your system. The PBT uses a chemical/electrical gauge (also referred to as a fuel cell), which determines your blood alcohol level. The law enforcement officer will place you under arrest if your blood alcohol level is 0.08 or more in the state of Minnesota. It is important to understand that this test is not admissible in court and only serves to enable the police officer to place you under arrest with probable cause for driving while impaired.

- The officer will read an implied consent advisory. During this time the officer will allow you to make a call to an attorney before you take any test. Your options are blood, breath or urine. The test may be suppressed, or not allowed in court, in the event that the police officer does not allow you to consult with the attorney of your choice, as long as you are actively trying and asking to speak with your attorney. Law enforcement preventing you from getting in touch with your attorney makes a conviction for a DWI much more difficult for the prosecutor.

- The law enforcement officer will then take you either to the hospital for a blood draw or to the police station for a urine or breath test.

- Once you have taken the test, one of several things might happen. You may be released to a sober adult, sent to a detoxification center or the police may request that you be kept in jail until your first appearance in court. Once in court, bail and release conditions will be set by the judge. In any case, you retain the right to take an alternative test administered by a person of your choosing, even if you are in jail.

In Minnesota if you have been arrested, released and charged with a DWI the time for action has started. Every DWI case in Minnesota consists of two distinct, but complex and significant cases: A criminal court case and an implied consent (IC), a civil court case. It is critical that an attorney litigate not only the criminal case, but also the implied consent as both cases can have separate and intertwined consequences. These consequences include, but are not limited to, jail time, fines, driver's license revocation, vehicle forfeiture and forfeiture of license plates. The implied consent needs to be filed with the court within 30 days of receiving notice if given a breath test or test refusal. If you take a blood or urine you have 33 days from the mailing date of the notice of license loss.

STOP OF THE MOTOR VEHICLE

Although no DWI cases are the same, many of the cases have similar legal issues to litigate. The legal examination of a case starts with the basis of the stop. An officer cannot stop a vehicle based upon a hunch or a whim. Rather, the officer must have made the stop based upon a violation of law no matter how slight.

There are two types of stops of a motor vehicle that commonly occur. The first type is an actual observation of driving conduct by an officer. In this context, the officer would follow the vehicle, notice what they believe is a violation of the law and then make a stop. The other common stop comes in the form of a 911 call. An individual will call 911 to report someone's driving conduct. An officer would then stop the vehicle based upon the report.

The importance of the stop cannot be stressed enough. If the officer makes contact with you and the judge does not deem the stop constitutional, the charges against you will be dismissed. It is because of this attorneys put a great deal of energy into investigating the reasons for the initial traffic stop or the initial contact with law enforcement.

Standardized Field Sobriety Tests

As I mentioned before, the officer will ask you to step out of the vehicle to perform a battery of standardized field sobriety tests. These tests are not mandatory and can be refused, although officers will never inform you of this.

Horizontal gaze nystagmus test or HGN is a test where the officer requests the individual follow a pen or their finger. The officer is looking for nystagmus or an involuntary jerking or bouncing of the eyeball that occurs. Horizontal gaze nystagmus (HGN) refers to a lateral or horizontal jerking when the eye gazes to the side. An officer is looking to see if the eyeball tracks left to right smoothly, if nystagmus occurs at a 45 degree angle and if nystagmus is present at maximum deviation, or your peripheral vision. In the impaired driving context, alcohol consumption or consumption of certain other central nervous system depressants like inhalants or phencyclidine, hinder the brain's ability to control eye muscles, therefore causing the jerk or bounce associated with HGN. As the degree of impairment becomes greater, the jerking or bouncing becomes more pronounced.

The 9 step walk and turn test is the second common test. For this test, an officer will have an individual stand with their hands at their side and one foot in front of the other standing heel-to-toe. While standing in this fashion, the officer will demonstrate walking 9 steps heel-to-toe on an imaginary line. After step 9 a turn will be made by making a series of small steps before making 9 steps back to where you originally started. The officer is not only concerned about how an individual performs on the test, but also how they listened to the directions.

The one leg stand consists of an individual standing on one leg with their arms at their side (up to 6 inches from body) counting to 30. The officer will provide directions prior to the individual starting the test. Again, the test is not only of the physical performance, but also how well directions are followed.

If the tests are preformed as trained in, a controlled setting they are up to 90% accurate in detecting an individual is intoxicated. Officers cannot perform the tests correctly 100% of the time as done in various studies. Furthermore, the tests performed by the officer are in the field not a classroom. Weather, area where the tests are completed, and individual's own medical and physical conditions all lead to the test being subject to harsh criticism.

Upon completion of the standardized field sobriety tests, the officer will request a PBT. The officer does not have to show you the results of the PBT.

The Arrest and the Implied Consent Advisory

Once the standardized field sobriety tests are completed, the officer will place an individual under arrest. Shortly after being placed under arrest, the officer will read a State provided document called an Implied Consent Advisory. The document informs an individual that they have been placed under arrest for DWI. The law requires them to take a test to determine their blood alcohol content. The implied consent advisory also outlines time to discuss with an attorney the arrest and subsequent requirements of taking a test. If an individual's right to counsel is violated then the results of the test cannot be used against them in court. A violation of the right to counsel includes not allowing you to use the telephone, and also not allowing you enough time to have a meaningful conversation with an attorney.

THE TESTS

Minnesota recognizes three types of tests that can be used in Court- breath, blood and urine.

The Breath Test

After years of litigation surrounding the Intoxilyzer 5000, the State of Minnesota has implemented the use of a new breath testing machine, the DataMaster DMT-G. The new breath testing device was purchased in hopes of effectively ending the use of the Intoxilyzer 5000 and the trouble surrounding the machine.

In 2010, the Bureau of Criminal Apprehension (BCA) spent approximately $1.7 million for 280 of the new DataMaster DMT-G devices. The DataMaster has large differences between the Intoxilyzer 5000. The DataMaster is designed to take two readings of a driver's blood-alcohol content at once, using two different methods. Although this sounds good, the BCA has informed law enforcement agencies it had shut off one of the testing methods. This request was based upon inconsistencies in the fuel cells.

The officer will turn on the machine and observe the individual for 15 minutes before taking the test. The officer is looking for a burp, belch or vomit that would raise the results of the test based upon mouth alcohol. The DataMaster will clear the machine with air and the first sample is given. The machine will clear itself again and run a test sample. The test sample must be within one-one hundredth of .08. Another sample is then given. The results will be the lower of the two samples and rounded down to the nearest hundredth.

The DataMaster is already in place and in use for most of the southern portion of Minnesota. It is off to a troublesome start based upon the errors that are being found and officers using the machine have received only limited training.

```
SUBJECT TEST

-------------------------
State of Minnesota
DataMaster DMT: 100503
Version: 208.206.205
-------------------------
Audit ID: 100503-571
Date: 07/05/2013
Time: 16:37:00
Location: Blue Earth Co. Jail

SUBJECT
Name:
License Number: 1971
State Of Issue: MN
DOB: 07/11/1961
Height: 5' 7"  Weight: 180
Gender: F

OPERATOR
Name: MELISSA M
Certificate Number: 514
Department:            PUBLIC SAFETY DEPT

ARRESTING OFFICER
Name: STEPHANIE
Arresting Department:
          PUBLIC SAFETY DEPT
Department ORI: MN0070100
County: BLUE EARTH
Type Of Test: TRAFFIC
Case Number / ICR Number: 13-18200
Commercial Vehicle: N
Observation Start Time: 4:22 PM
Observed By: OFFICER W        3121

CONTROL INFORMATION
Lot Number: 30212080A1
Control Target: 0.076
Expiration: 12/01/2014

DIAGNOSTIC CHECK                PASSED  16:37
AIR BLANK                        0.000  16:39
SUBJECT SAMPLE                Vol=1.75  16:39
  IR = 0.359
AIR BLANK                        0.000  16:41
CONTROL SAMPLE                          16:41
  IR = 0.074
AIR BLANK                        0.000  16:43
SUBJECT SAMPLE                Vol=2.46  16:43
  IR = 0.353
AIR BLANK                        0.000  16:44

*************************************
REPORTED VALUE IN g/210L      0.35  16:43
*************************************

REMARKS:
Long steady breaths
Two mouth pieces
No BBV

Operator Signature
```

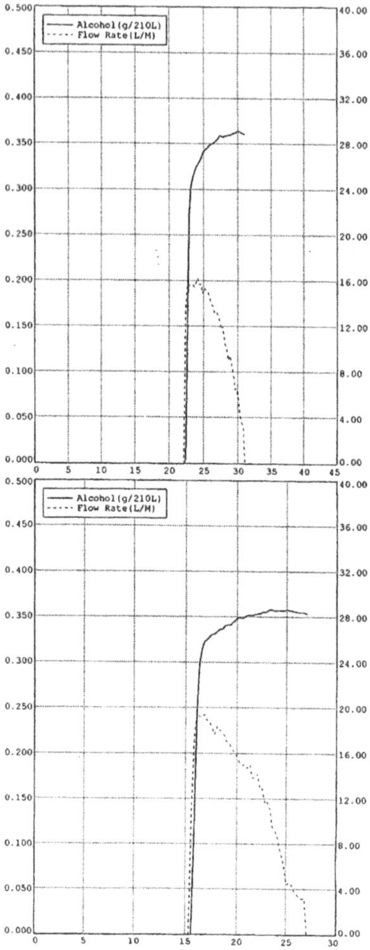

Fig. 1 An example of a DataMaster test result

The Blood Test

If a blood sample is offered, the officer will transport you to the nearest hospital for a blood draw. The individual taking the blood should use a non-alcohol wipe. Two vials of blood are drawn. The blood must be drawn into vacuum sealed containers to end fermentation of blood. The test is sent to the BCA to be analyzed. Test results will normally be returned in 6-8 weeks. Below is a blood sample report from the BCA that you would receive by mail.

MINNESOTA DEPARTMENT OF PUBLIC SAFETY
Bureau of Criminal Apprehension
Forensic Science Laboratory - St. Paul
1430 Maryland Avenue East
St. Paul, MN 55106
TEL: (651) 793-2900 TTY: (651) 282-6555 FAX: (651) 793-2901
An ASCLD/LAB-*International* Accredited Laboratory

To: Eagle Lake Police Department
705 Parkway Ave
Eagle Lake, MN 56024

Lab No. S11-13654
Report No. 1

Attention: Officer John Kopp

REPORT ON THE EXAMINATION OF PHYSICAL EVIDENCE
Toxicology 09/28/2011

Laboratory Number:	S11-13654	**Requesting Agency:**	
Section Reporting:	Toxicology	**Agency Case Number:**	
Case Type:	DWI	**County:**	Blue Earth
Principal:		**Date of Birth:**	

Description of Submitted Evidence:

Item	Type and Packaging	Kit Number	Description/Source	Date/Time Collected
1	Sealed BCA DWI blood collection kit	B347017		08/31/2011 00:40

Results of Laboratory Examination:

Analysis revealed an ethyl alcohol concentration of 0.08 grams per 100 milliliters of blood.

Pursuant to Minn. Statute 634.15, I have analyzed at the Minnesota Bureau of Criminal Apprehension Forensic Science Laboratory, using an approved gas chromatographic procedure, this sealed sample of blood identified to me as having been obtained from the above individual. I hereby certify that I am trained in the analysis and interpretation of blood and urine tests for alcohol pursuant to Minn. Rule 7502.0600 and that the above is true and accurate.

Donna B Zittel

Donna B. Zittel, FTS-ABFT
Forensic Scientist

Disposition: This evidence will be destroyed by the laboratory twelve months following the date of this report. Please notify the BCA Forensic Science Laboratory if you would like the evidence returned to your agency.

Distribution:Eagle Lake Police Department - 1

Fig 2. Example of a blood test report

The Urine Test

A urine test will be given at the jail. The officer will open a package and hand a cup with white powder at the bottom to you. A male or female officer will be there to observe. The powder is to preserve the sample and end fermentation. The sample is sent to the BCA to be analyzed. The test results, just like the blood test, will be returned in approximately 6-8 weeks.

If offered a blood test, an individual can opt for a urine test and vice a versa.

MINNESOTA DEPARTMENT OF PUBLIC SAFETY
Bureau of Criminal Apprehension
Forensic Science Laboratory - St. Paul
1430 Maryland Avenue East
St. Paul, MN 55106
TEL: (651) 793-2900 TTY: (651) 282-6555 FAX: (651) 793-2901
An ASCLD/LAB-*International* Accredited Laboratory

'o: Sleepy Eye Police Department
130 Second Avenue NW
Sleepy Eye, MN 56085

Lab No. S12-00900
Report No. 1

Attention: Justin Bauer

REPORT ON THE EXAMINATION OF PHYSICAL EVIDENCE
Toxicology 01/30/2012

Laboratory Number:	S12-00900	**Requesting Agency:**	
Section Reporting:	Toxicology	**Agency Case Number:**	
Case Type:	DWI	**County:**	Brown
Principals:		**Date of Birth:**	

Description of Submitted Evidence:

Item	Type and Packaging	Kit Number	Description/Source	Date/Time Collected
1	Sealed BCA DWI urine collection kit	U192816		01/14/2012 22:43

Results of Laboratory Examination:

Analysis revealed an ethyl alcohol concentration of 0.16 grams per 67 milliliters of urine.

Pursuant to Minn. Statute 634.15, I have analyzed at the Minnesota Bureau of Criminal Apprehension Forensic Science Laboratory, using an approved gas chromatographic procedure, this sealed sample of urine identified to me as having been obtained from the abo individual. I hereby certify that I am trained in the analysis and interpretation of blood and urine tests for alcohol pursuant to Minn. 7502.0600 and that the above is true and accurate.

Mumtaz S. Pasha

Mumtaz S. Pasha. Ph.D.
Forensic Scientist

Disposition: This evidence will be destroyed by the laboratory twelve months following the date of this report. Please notify the BCA Forensic Science Laboratory if you would like the evidence returned to your agency.

Distribution:Sleepy Eye Police Department - 1

Fig. 3 Example of a urine test report

Refusal

If a test is not taken, an individual will be charged with test refusal. A person can also be charged with a refusal, if the officer does not believe they are actively trying to submit a breath sample into the DataMaster, essentially faking it, or if the two samples are not within one-one hundredth of .08.

An officer may hold an individual until a hearing can take place without receiving test results.

WHAT IS MY CHARGE?

In Minnesota, the Prosecutor can look back 10 years in your record to determine if you have been convicted of a DWI or have lost your driver's license due to being intoxicated while driving. The judge will also be notified of any such events that might have happened longer than in the past 10 years. This "10 year look back" is used to determine the level of the charge.The lowest level of DWI is 4th degree, which is a misdemeanor. It is punishable by up to 90 days in jail and/or a fine of up to a $1,000.00. If an aggravating factor exists, commonly prior convictions, the charge will increase to a 3rd degree DWI or a 2nd degree DWI. A third offense within 10 years or a DWI is a 2nddegree DWI. A 2nddegree DWI is punishable by 365 days of jail and/or a $3,000 fine.

Both are a gross misdemeanor, punishable by up to 365 days jail and/or a $3,000.00 fine.

Four DWI convictions in 10 years will result in a felony DWI charge. First Degree DWI is punishable by up to seven years imprisonment and/or a fine of up to $14,000.

With each enhanced charge, Minnesota Statutes require a mandatory minimum jail sentence. Below are the mandatory minimum sentences for DWIs in Minnesota:

# OF Prior DWIs w/in 10 years	Fine	Minimum jail
0	**Up to $1,000**	**Up to 90 Days**
1	**Up to $3,000**	**30 days**
2	**Up to $3,000**	**90 days**
3	**Up to $7,000**	**180 days**
4	**Up to $14,000**	**365 days**

The criminal penalties for convicted DWI offenders in Minnesota can be extreme. They range from no jail time and a low fine up to 7 years in prison. Every county in Minnesota has different recommended sentences for driving while impaired.

AGGRAVATING FACTORS

An aggravated or enhanced DWI is the charge of 3rd degree DWI, 2nd degree DWI or a 1st degree DWI. For a charge of DWI to be aggravated, one of the following factors must take place:

1. A test result of .20 or more;

2. A child was in the vehicle at the time of the stop;

3. A prior DWI or an alcohol license loss in the past10 years or;

4. A refusal of the blood, breath or urine test.

Aggravating factors will lead to mandatory bail situations, and in most cases waiting in jail until able to be heard by a Judge.

A criminal complaint or a "tab charge" will be given to the defendant informing him or her of the charges. This is unlike a fourth degree DWI where an individual will receive a ticket or a letter indicating when court is.

BAIL

In Minnesota, mandatory bail is required by Minnesota Statute if test results are over .20, a child was in the vehicle, or if there was a conviction of a prior DWI in the past 10 years. Statute requires bail to be set at $12,000.00. Due to this mandatory bail, a defendant must appear before a judge prior to being released. It is common that the judge will agree to release the defendant as long as they are willing to be subject to an alcohol testing device. These devices are called EHM (electronic home monitoring) or SCRAM, (secure continuous remote alcohol monitor).

The EHM device is attached to a telephone and provides a continuous signaling radio frequency, visual verification and remote breath alcohol testing technologies in one fully integrated unit. It gathers a deep lung sample to provide an accurate confirmation of alcohol ingestion, and renders a quantitative alcohol level, not just pass or fail.

The SCRAM device is worn on the ankle and measures the subject's blood alcohol level through perspiration on the skin. The measurement of transdermal alcohol content is converted into a blood alcohol level.

Both of these devices cost about $10 to $20.00 a day for use. Grants are available in some counties if you qualify.

WHAT ARE "CONDITIONS OF RELEASE" FROM JAIL?

Conditions of release are requirements set by the Court that an individual must follow to remain out of jail. The conditions are set at the first appearance and can be modified by request at any later hearing.

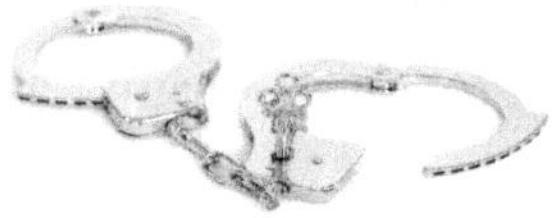

Common conditions of release include:

1. No use or possession of alcohol or other mood altering chemicals;
2. Random testing upon request;
3. Curfew;
4. Subject to GPS mentoring;
5. Subject to alcohol monitoring; and
6. Subject to random searches of one's place ofresidence or vehicle.

If these conditions are violated, an arrest warrant is issued. It is not unforeseen for a probation officer to stop by an individual's home to ensure the conditions are being followed. What this means is if the judge ordered no possession of alcohol and your significant other or roommate has beer in the fridge, it needs to be removed from the home or apartment.

COURT HEARINGS

After the first appearance, the Court will set conditions of release and ensure the defendant is aware of their rights. The next hearing is called either an Omnibus or a Pre-trial, depending on the level of offense. An Omnibus or Pre-trial Hearing is held to determine that each party has completed discovery, and if a contested hearing is needed. Generally these hearings take only 15 minutes and it will not be necessary for you to testify; however, your attendance is required. Initially these hearings are helpful because it provides an opportunity to speak directly with the prosecuting attorney to get your case resolved or a trial date is set.

If the case is not settled a Contested Omnibus or contested pre-trial is held. In this hearing, testimony is taken. The testimony can be offered from the officer, witness or you. This hearing usually lasts about 30 minutes.

After the contested hearing the judge will need to make a determination if the charges can continue or what evidence can be used at trial. The judge will normally request a written legal argument called a legal brief. A ruling will be made within 90 days from the last submission from to the court.

The next step is a trial. About only 1% of cases ever go to trial.

CRIMINAL CASE CHART OF HEARINGS

The flow chart on the next page depicts the series of hearings that take place in a Criminal case.

Arraignment/Rule 8 Hearing

Set conditions of Release
(Bail, Home Monitoring, Contact restrictions, cannot leave state)

Pre-Trial/Omnibus Hearing

Inform Judge of issues in the case
File Motions for a Contested Hearing
Insure Discovery is complete

Sentencing Hearing

Judge imposes sentence
Examples – Probation, Jail, Fine, Classes, Restitution

Plea Hearing

Inform Judge of Agreement
File Guilty Plea Petition
Judge may request Pre-Sentence Investigation for Sentencing purposes

Pre-Trial/Trial
Settlement offer discussed
OR
Attend Jury Trial hearing

Contested Pre-Trial/Omnibus Hearing
Officer/witness put on stand to testify
Legal Arguments made

PRE-SENTENCE INVESTIGATION OR "PSI"

The PSI is a meeting between yourself and a probation agent during which you will be given the opportunity to explain things as you see them and put your version of events on record. PSI meetings can be extremely intimidating and stressful for you, as the probation agent will

also be asking you a lot of questions and putting your answers in writing. It is your attorney's responsibility to prepare you for this meeting and take whatever time is necessary to ensure you understand what is involved, what to expect and how to navigate through it. Depending on the probation agent assigned to your case, your meeting should last about an hour. Some agents take longer, some take less time, and the length of the meeting will also depend on the specifics of your case. A few weeks after your meeting, the probation agent will send his or her written recommendation on what your punishment, fine or sentence should be, both to the Judge, prosecutor and your attorney. As soon as your lawyer receives this document, it is his or her responsibility to share it with you, review it and ensure you understand it, and discuss the next steps.

SENTENCING

At sentencing, the prosecutor may make a recommendation to the Court about the sentence. After the prosecutor's recommendation, your attorney will have an opportunity to make a statement on the behalf of their client. Letters of recommendation can also be provided to the court from treatment providers, AA members and family and friends that support the defendant as well. Finally, the defendant can make a statement or exercise their right to allocution, or addressing the court with a statement. I believe it is very important that a defendant makes a statement. The statement does not have to be overly lengthy (around 30 to 60 seconds is perfect). This statement should help the judge understand the circumstances surrounding the event, what has taken place since to ensure it was a one-time mistake, and how this case has affected not only the defendant but also friends and family of the defendant. The judge will review the Pre-Sentence Investigation report (if ordered) and pronounce a sentence at that time.

The sentence must be within minimum or maximum limits set by statute. If the offense resulted in injury to another person or damage to another person's property, the defendant may be required to make restitution. Restitution is the amount of money the defendant must pay to the victim of the defendant's crime to cover costs for treatment of an injury, or to repair or replace property damaged by the defendant.

PROBATION

In most cases, probation will be a condition of the sentence. A probation agent will be assigned to the case.

1. Common probation requirements are:Jail will either be executed jail (jail that one must serve) or a stayed jail sentence (jail that will only be required if a probation violation takes place).

2. A chemical use assessment and follow all recommendations;

3. MADD victim impact panel; and

4. Abstain from all mood altering chemicals.

Alternative Punishments to Jail When Facing DWI

Minnesota law requires mandatory jail if charged with a third degree DWI or higher. There are alternatives to mandatory jail. In lieu of jail, people can qualify for the ignition interlock program. That would permit the courts to waive the mandatory minimum jail time. Some counties will allow you to do EHM, (Electronic Home Monitoring) or house arrest. Other counties will require community or sentence to serve (STS) in lieu of jail time.

Motor Vehicle Forfeiture

In many DWI cases the police or sheriff's department has the authority to seize and forfeit (take and then sell) your motor vehicle. Vehicle forfeiture is covered by Minnesota Statute §169A.63. It is important to know that the offense includes both DWI offenses and alcohol-related driver's license revocations arising from separate incidents. The motor vehicle used in a DWI offense may be seized and forfeited by the police under the following circumstances:

1. The current offense is the 3rd offense within 10 years and the driver is now charged with another DWI or test refusal. (Second Degree DWI).

2. The current offense is the 2nd offense within 10 years and the driver is now charged with another DWI with a child under the age of 16 present, or driving with an alcohol level of 0.20% or more. (Second Degree DWI).

3. The current offense is the fourth offense within 10 years and the driver is now charged with felony DWI. (First Degree DWI).

4. The driver is charged with a DWI or test refusal while the driver's license is under cancellation for being inimical to public safety.

5. The driver is charged with a DWI or test refusal while the driver's license is subject to a restriction prohibiting consumption of any amount of alcohol or controlled substance (B-Card restriction).

The police can seize the vehicle immediately and keep possession of it while the criminal and forfeiture cases are pending. The arresting agency must issue a Notice of Seizure and Intent to Forfeit the Vehicle to the driver of the vehicle and to anyone else who may have an ownership or possessory interest in the vehicle and it MUST be done within 30 days of the forfeiture.

There are some defenses available, such as a motor vehicle is subject to forfeiture under this law only if its owner knew or should have known of the unlawful use of the vehicle. If the driver is the owner, or one of joint owners, then this not a defense. However, if the vehicle is owned by someone who was not present when the DWI occurred and who had no knowledge that the driver would use it to violate this law, the owner has a legal defense against the forfeiture action.

This demand for a hearing to determine the legality of the forfeiture must be made within 30 days to be effective or else the owner of the vehicle will lose the vehicle no matter what the outcome of the criminal case may be.

IMPAIRED OPERATION Ticket or Case No.

NOTICE OF SEIZURE AND INTENT TO FORFEIT VEHICLE Court 5th District

DL

To (Recipient of Notice): First Middle Last DOB

Address: Street City State Zip

VEHICLE: MN

Make Year VIN/HIN/Serial No. License/Registration No./State

Location/Date/Time Seized

Description/Type of Vehicle: ATV ____ Snowmobile ____ Motorboat ____ Other Car

ADMINISTRATIVE FORFEITURE NOTICE

YOU ARE HEREBY NOTIFIED, pursuant to Minnesota Statutes, Section 169A.63, that the vehicle listed above was used in the commission of a designated offense or was used in conduct resulting in a designated license revocation.

Forfeiture of the property is automatic unless within 30 days of receipt of this form you demand a judicial determination of this matter. The procedure for obtaining a judicial determination is set out in Minnesota Statutes, Section 169A.63, Subdivision 8 on the reverse side of this form. IF YOU DO NOT DEMAND JUDICIAL REVIEW EXACTLY AS PRESCRIBED IN MINNESOTA STATUTES, SECTION 169A.63, SUBDIVISION 8, YOU LOSE THE RIGHT TO A JUDICIAL DETERMINATION OF THIS FORFEITURE AND YOU LOSE ANY RIGHT YOU MAY HAVE TO THE ABOVE DESCRIBED PROPERTY. YOU MAY NOT HAVE TO PAY THE FILING FEE FOR THE DEMAND IF DETERMINED YOU ARE UNABLE TO AFFORD THE FEE. IF THE PROPERTY IS WORTH $7,500 OR LESS, YOU MAY FILE YOUR CLAIM IN CONCILIATION COURT. YOU DO NOT HAVE TO PAY THE CONCILIATION COURT FILING FEE IF THE PROPERTY IS WORTH LESS THAN $500.

Yam khoom tsoom fwv muab lawm yuav cia li poob rau tuag yog hais tias nyob rau hauv 30 hnub tom qab uas tau txais daim ntawv no koj tsis hais kom muaj kev soj ntsuam raws li txoj cai lij choj nrog taug tus tsob thoom no. Tus txheej txheem hais kom muaj kev soj ntsuam raws li txoj cai lij choj yeej muaj sau tseg rau hauv Kev Cai Minnesota Tshooj 169A.63, Dib 8 nyob rau daim ntawv no sab nraud. YOG HAIS TIAS KOJ TSIS THOV KOM MUAJ KEV SOJ NTSUAM RAWS LI TXOJ CAI LIJ CHOJ RAWS NRAIM LI UAS TAU PIAV TSEG RAU HAUV KEV CAI MINNESOTA, TSHOOJ 169A.63, DIB 8, KOJ YUAV TSIS MUAJ CAI HAIS KOM MUAJ KEV SOJ NTSUAM RAWS LI TXOJ CAI LIJ CHOJ HAIS TXOG YAM KHOOM TSOOM FWV MUAB LAWM, THIAB KOJ YUAV POOB TAG TXHUA TXOJ CAI HAIS TXOG COV KHOOM UAS TAU TEEV LOS SAUM NO. KOJ YUAV TSIS RAUG THEM TUS NQI UA NTAUB NTAWV HAIS YOG TIAS MUAB NTSUAM XYUAS LOS TXOG KOJ YUAV THEM TSIS TAUS. YOG QHOV KHOOM NTAWD RAUG NQI TSAWG TSHAJ LOS YOG RAUG NQI TXOG LI $7,500 NYIAJ, CES KOJ MUS UA TAU NTAUB NTAWV HAIS HAUV CHAW HAIS PLAUB ME (CONCILIATION COURT). KOJ YUAV TSIS RAUG THEM TUS NQI UA NTAUB NTAWV HAIS HAUV CHAW HAIS PLAUB ME YOG HAIS TIAS YAM KHOOM NTAWD RAUG NQI TSAWG TSHAJ $500 NYIAJ.

El decomiso de esto bienes es automático, excepto cuándo pida una determinación judicial de este asunto dentro de un periodo de 30 días después de haber recibido este aviso. El procedimiento para obtener una determinación judicial se establece en los estatutos de Minnesota, sección 169A.63, subdivisión 8, que aparece impreso al reverso de esta formulario. SI USTED NO PIDE UNA REVISIÓN JUDICIAL EXACTAMENTE TAL Y COMO SE PRESCRIBE EN LOS ESTATUTOS DE MINNESOTA, SECCIÓN 169A.63, SUBDIVISIÓN 8, PERDERÁ TODO DERECHO A UNA DETERMINACIÓN JUDICIAL DE ESTE DECOMISO Y TODOS LOS DERECHOS QUE PUEDA TENER SOBRE LAS PROPIEDADES DESCRITAS ANTERIORMENTE. ES POSIBLE QUE NO TENGA QUE PAGAR LA TASA JUDICIAL DE LA DEMANDA SI SE DETERMINA QUE NO TIENE MEDIOS PARA HACERLO. SI EL VALOR DEL BIEN MUEBLE NO EXCEDE LOS $7,500 DÓLARES, USTED PUEDE HACER UNA RECLAMACIÓN EN EL TRIBUNAL DE CONCILIACIÓN. NO TIENE QUE PAGAR LA TASA JUDICIAL PARA EL TRIBUNAL DE CONCILIACIÓN SI EL VALOR DEL BIEN MUEBLE ES DE HASTA 500 DÓLARES.

PEACE OFFICER CERTIFICATE OF SERVICE

I certify that on (date) 12-18-11 I gave a true copy of this notice to the person named above at (location of service) Brown County Law Enforcement Center - Jail and have seized the above described property for forfeiture.

Signature of Officer [signature] Officer's Printed Name Charles Rauche

310 12-18-11 New Ulm Police Department

Badge No. Dated Law Enforcement Agency

Notice received by X Check if recipient refused to sign ☐

ORIGINAL COPY to Prosecuting Attorney YELLOW COPY to Claimant PINK COPY to Law Enforcement Agency

© 8/2005 Minnesota County Attorneys Association

B-CARD/ CANCELED IPS

If an individual has 2 prior DWI license losses within a 10 year period or 3 in a lifetime, the new license revocation will result in a cancelation of driving privileges as inimical to public safety (IPS). Prior to having driving privileges reinstated a person must demonstrate that they have complete chemical dependency treatment and any aftercare. The process for reinstatement is determined by rules set out by the Minnesota Department of Public Safety (DPS).

The new license will outlaw any consumption of alcohol. If a person with IPS status is found drinking alcohol at any time their license can be revoked. It cannot be stressed enough that IPS status does not only prohibit drinking alcohol and driving but it prohibits any consumption of alcohol.

DRIVER AND VEHICLE SERVICES DIVISION
445 MINNESOTA ST., SUITE 180
ST. PAUL, MINNESOTA 55101-5180
(651) 296-2025 TTY (651) 282-6555

PAGE: 1
MAILING DATE: 01/10/12
RB3

STATE OF MINNESOTA
DEPARTMENT OF PUBLIC SAFETY
SAINT PAUL 55101

DS CODE:
DOB :

UNDER THE AUTHORITY OF AND AS DIRECTED BY THE LAWS OF THE STATE OF MINNESOTA YOUR MINNESOTA DRIVER'S LICENSE OR PRIVILEGE TO OPERATE A MOTOR VEHICLE IS HEREBY REVOKED EFFECTIVE 01-20-12.

REASON FOR WITHDRAWAL:
ALCOHOL CONCENTRATION WAS .08 OR MORE.
12-18-11

REQUIREMENTS FOR REINSTATEMENT:
* WITHDRAWAL OF ALL PRIVILEGES EFFECTIVE ON ABOVE DATE AND TO CONTINUE FOR 3 YEARS.
CANCEL AND DENY 171.04
* PASS THE DWI/DRUG WRITTEN TEST.
* PAY $680 REINSTATEMENT FEE.
* MAKE APPLICATION FOR NEW LICENSE.
* SUBMIT EVIDENCE OF SUCCESSFUL REHABILITATION FROM CHEMICAL DEPENDENCY.
* COMPLETE THE IGNITION INTERLOCK DEVICE PROGRAM.

ONCE YOUR DRIVING PRIVILEGES ARE UNDER WITHDRAWAL, YOU MAY NOT DRIVE AGAIN IN MINNESOTA UNDER ANY CONDITION, INCLUDING USING A DRIVER'S LICENSE FROM ANOTHER JURISDICTION OR A LIMITED LICENSE FROM MINNESOTA ISSUED FOR A PREVIOUS WITHDRAWAL. WHEN WE HAVE RECEIVED VERIFICATION THAT YOU HAVE COMPLETED ALL REINSTATEMENT REQUIREMENTS, AND YOU HAVE RECEIVED A NOTICE OF REINSTATEMENT FROM THIS DEPARTMENT, YOU MAY DRIVE IN MINNESOTA.

REINSTATEMENT FEES MAY BE PAID AT ANY DRIVER'S LICENSE EXAMINATION STATION IN MINNESOTA, OR IN PERSON AT THE DRIVER EVALUATION OFFICE, 445 MINNESOTA STREET, SUITE 170, ST. PAUL, MINNESOTA, OR THROUGH THE MAIL BY SENDING A CHECK OR MONEY ORDER TO THE ADDRESS LISTED AT THE TOP OF THIS PAGE. CHECKS SHOULD BE MADE PAYABLE TO DRIVER AND VEHICLE SERVICES . A $30.00 FEE IS ASSESSED FOR DISHONORED CHECKS (MINNESOTA STATUTE 604.113, SUBDIVISION 2).

IGNITION INTERLOCK

IF YOUR LICENSE HAS BEEN REVOKED, YOU MAY BE ELIGIBLE TO PARTICIPATE IN THE IGNITION INTERLOCK PROGRAM UNDER MINNESOTA STATUTE, SECTION 171.306. DRIVERS THAT ARE CANCELED AND DENIED AS INIMICAL TO PUBLIC SAFETY DUE TO MULTIPLE DWI OFFENSES ARE REQUIRED TO INSTALL AN IGNITION INTERLOCK DEVICE PRIOR TO OBTAINING DRIVING PRIVILEGES.
FOR MORE INFORMATION, CALL (651) 296-2948
OR VISIT HTTP://DVS.DPS.MN.GOV

REQUEST FOR ADMINISTRATIVE REVIEW

OVER

DVLTTR (REV. 8/00)

Implied Consent And Contesting Your Driver's License Suspension

As discussed earlier, when you are arrested for DWI there are two distinct cases, the criminal case and the implied consent. A judicial request for an implied consent hearing must be made 30 days after receiving notice of revocation of your license (33 days if notice is mailed). The document that precedes this page is a sample letter that the DPS will send you.

The implied consent affects license revocation license status, and issuance of special plates (i.e. whiskey plates). First time DWI with the offense with a blood alcohol content under .16 will receive a 90 day revocation. After being without a license for 15 days an individual can apply for a work permit. If the alcohol test is over.16 the revocation period increases to 1 year. No limited license will be issued. Rather, to drive legally, an ignition interlock device would need to be installed in the vehicle. Ironically, if you refuse to take a test you can have a work permit issued after 15 days of license loss, but that would include remaining on the work permit for the duration of a year or using ignition interlock.

The second offense carries a one-year license revocation if the test is under a .16. If it is over .16, a two year revocation would take effect.

It is important to remember the test we are talking about the results of the evidentiary test. This test is not taken in the field but rather in the police station or at the hospital. This is always a blood, breath or urine test.

		Revocation Period	Hard Revocation Period	Limited License (Work Permit) Available	Required Sober Period-Interlock Required	Current Revocation Period
1st Offense	Under 16	90 Days	0 Days with Interlock 15 Days if no Interlock	Yes	None	90 Days
	Refusel	1 Year	0 Days with Interlock 15 Days if no Interlock	Yes	None	1 Year; 90 if plea to DUI
	0.16	1 year	0 Days with Interlock 1 Year if no Interlock	No	None	180 Days (.20)
2nd Offense	Under .16	1 Year	0 Days with Interlock 1 Year if no Interlock	No	None	180 Days
	.16 +	2 Year	0 Days with Interlock 2 Year if no Interlock	No	None	365 Days (.20)
3rd Offense		3 Year	30 Day before Interlock Eligible	Yes, for the first year of sobriety	3 Years of proof of sobriety before eligible for unrestricted driving privileges	1 Year
4th Offense		4 Year	30 Day before Interlock Eligible	Yes, for the first year of sobriety	4 Years of proof of sobriety before eligible for unrestricted driving privileges	3 Years
5th Offense or more		6 Year	30 Day before Interlock Eligible	Yes, for the first year of sobriety	6 Years of proof of sobriety before eligible for unrestricted driving privileges	6 Years

THE IMPLIED CONSENT HEARING

An implied consent is a civil hearing that the Attorney General must prove by clear and convincing evidence that the driver of the vehicle had a blood alcohol content of over .08 or over .16. The hearing takes place in front of a judge without a jury. The hearing needs to take place within 60 days from the date of license loss. If the hearing is not held within the 60 days, a temporary license will be given to the driver.

For many people, they cannot tell the difference between the criminal contested hearing and the implied consent. In fact, most attorneys will have both cases take place at the same time. The Attorney General will call the officer(s) that made the arrest and possibly additional witnesses from the BCA.

An implied consent hearing is limited in scope. A Judge can only hear the following issues:

- Did the peace officer have probable cause to believe the person was driving, operating or in physical control of a motor vehicle or commercial vehicle?

- Was the person lawfully placed under arrest?

- Was the person involved in a motor vehicle accident or collision resulting in property damage, personal injury or death?
- Did the person refuse to take a screening test (A PBT)?

- If the screening test was administered, did the test indicate an alcohol concentration of 0.08 or more?

- At the time of the request for the test, did the peace officer inform the person of the person's rights and the consequences of taking or refusing the test as required?

- Did the person refuse to permit the test?

- If a test was taken by a person driving, operating or in physical control of a motor vehicle, did the test results indicate at the time of testing:
  - an alcohol concentration of 0.08 or more; or
  - the presence of a controlled substance?

- If a test was taken by a person driving, operating or in physical control of a commercial motor vehicle, did the test results indicate an alcohol concentration of 0.04 or more at the time of testing?

- Was the testing method used valid and reliable and were the test results accurately evaluated?

BUT WHAT IF I NEED TO DRIVE NOW??

In 2011 Minnesota began a program allowing individuals with a DWI license loss the ability to drive. In most case the day they lose their license with the assistance of ignition interlock. An "ignition interlock device" is a small PBT (portable breath test) which measures the blood-alcohol level of an automobile driver and is required before starting the car. To use the device, a driver must blow into a small tube before starting the car. If the driver fails the tests, the car will not start, and additional revocation periods may result. The machine also requires rolling starts. Rolling starts are tests while the operator is driving the vehicle. Rolling starts commonly take place every eight minutes to a half hour to continue driving.

Minnesota requires the offender to pay for the rental and installation of the device and the costs can be substantial. The device can be embarrassing; as it must be operated each and every time the driver gets in the car.

WHISKY PLATES – SPECIAL-ISSUE DRUNK DRIVER LICENSE PLATES

Whiskey plates or special issued plates will be issued for a first time DWI offender over .16 and for subsequent violations within a 10 year period. The plates are distinctive consisting of a white background with black or blue print if it is an older plate. The license plate will remain on the vehicle for one year past your renewal period.

The special license plates are on your car and everyone knows that you are facing DWI charges or you are a convicted "drunk driver". An officer cannot stop a vehicle based upon the license plates, but commonly the drivers with the special issued plates get stopped more often for minor traffic violations.

Should You Journal What Happened To You Before, During And After You Are Arrested?

After your release it is important to document what happened. Specifically, recall the date of incident and where the incident took place. An attorney will also ask questions about why the officer made contact with

you. Was it based on driving conduct such as speeding, weaving or swerving? How did you feel you faired on the field sobriety tests? Did the officer perform the normal battery of tests consisting of HGN, one leg stand and the 9 step walk and turn? What were the weather conditions? Were you allowed to contact an attorney during the implied consent advisory? Did the officer give you enough time?

It is important to talk to your attorney about any medical problems that you may have as well.

How A DWI Conviction Affects Your Auto And Life Insurance

Once a conviction of a DWI is entered, an auto insurance increase is to be expected. Many insurance companies will take the DWI into account for approximately 3-5 years. The 3 to 5 years starts running

from the date of incident. For example if John Smith was arrested for a DWI on January 1st, but the case was not completed until December 31st, Mr. Smith's insurance would not increase until December 31st.

The increase remains for 2-4 years. This additional time saved him one year of increased insurance rates.

Not only does your auto insurance increase, but also life insurance. Due to the conviction, many life insurance companies believe that this is an indication of being involved in risky behaviors.

The Low Cost Attorneys And Why Experience Matters

Many attorneys have opened their own firm directly out of law school due to the economic downturn. This has led to aggressive price slashing among inexperienced attorneys. The old saying "you get what you pay for," is tried and true.

There are two options on how attorney's bill. The first option is that an attorney will charge a retainer and deduct their hourly rate for every hour they work. The pro is that it normally costs less to begin the case. The con is that it commonly costs more in the long run. If you are wanting to aggressively fight the charges against you or be informed of your case, this option ends up costing more.

The other option is a flat fee or capped retainer. The attorney will quote a retainer amount that will cover all of the attorney's fees. If the client would reach an agreement on their case early, then any unused amount of the retainer would be returned. Clients prefer the flat fee due to the fact that it is a set price.

Help You Help Yourself

After you have retained an attorney, it is critical that the client becomes informed and invested in their case and asks questions. As part of the process, this includes reading police reports, setting up an appointment to discuss the reports and watching the arrest video. Another request I make to clients is to get a chemical use assessment and follow the recommendations. Finally, once released, follow the conditions of release.

WILL MY ARREST BE PUBLIC?

An arrest record is public information. How public the information becomes generally depends upon the charges. Normally, on a first time DWI, the smaller towns will print the arrest record in the paper. If the charge requires bail, then the publicity is not from the arrest record, but rather the online jail roster.

If you have the designer license plates,(i.e. whiskey plates,) co-workers figure out fairly quickly that something happened.

Weighing The Consequences Of Pleading Guilty To The First Offense

When people are charged with a DWI for the first time, often they plead guilty in hopes they do not have to deal with it. The reality is that a DWI can be a life and career changing moment. The first mistake, especially on a first time DWI, is collateral consequences. Those are the consequences that flow from a conviction. People may plead guilty without understanding the license loss, possibility of jail, or understand the requirements of fines, probation, and restrictions. If you retain an attorney these consequences can often be mitigated. The other issue comes down to insurance. Normally an insurance company will not raise your rates until you are convicted.

How Are DWI Defendant's Treated By The Court System And How Can You Help?

When someone is in front of a judge in court they have tremendous trepidation. This is normal. The State has highly trained and aggressive attorneys with endless resources. The playing field does not feel level. There are things a defendant can do to help shine a better light on them. First and foremost a chemical use assessment. A chemical use assessment is an assessment done by a chemical abuse counselor to determine if an individual has a use or abuse problem. The assessment consists of a meeting with the counselor and verification of the information by two collateral sources provided by the client. Once the assessment is complete recommendations are made. By completing a chemical use assessment as soon as possible, it not only shows the court that you are serious about the charges and your sobriety, but also allows your attorney to argue for less strenuous conditions of release due to the proactive approach. When you are potentially dealing with mandatory bail of

$12,000.00, this simple step can make all of the difference in the world.

What Do CDL (Commercial Driver's License) Holders Face?

A CDL makes an already difficult situation more complex. Minnesota does not issue work permits that would allow for the use of the CDL. Unfortunately, if you are convicted of a DWI in Minnesota (or in any state for that matter) Federal Regulation 383.51 will be triggered. In a nutshell, a DWI conviction will result in a one (1) year ban on your CDL. A second conviction will result in a lifetime ban on obtaining a commercial driver license. This is true even if you are in a vehicle such as your private car, SUV, boat or motorcycle.

In 2008, the law changed. Currently, if you are found not guilty of the DWI charge or it is reduced to a careless driving charge, and you lost your driver's license, you will face the same loss of your CDL as if you had been convicted. This is why it is important to file the Implied Consent Petition to attempt to keep this from going on your record.

PRIVATE ATTORNEY VS. A PUBLIC DEFENDER

Many individuals who find themselves charged with a DWI have to make a decision on whether they will hire private counsel or request a public defender. The attorney who represents an individual is one of the most important decisions in a case.

So what are the differences?

When charged with a DWI along with other criminal charges, the State has also implemented a civil lawsuit case or the implied consent. Since this is not a criminal action, a public defender does not represent an individual for this case but private counsel would. For many the implied consent has more of an effect on everyday life then the criminal case ever would.

Another distinction between a public defender and a private attorney is the number of open cases a public defender has at any given time. In a recent article by Minnesota Public Radio, Jessica Major followed a public defender for a day. What she found out is that on average a client gets to spend about 12 minutes with their public defender because of their caseload. Due to the current budget shortage this is not the exception to the rule, but rather the reality of the situation. While public defenders are many times exceptional legal minds, due to the time crunch they cannot give the personal attention to a client as one would expect.

Hard work and extra time on a file can translate into a better outcome for a client. In a New York Times article in 2007, Emory University found that a criminal defendant charged with a serious crime who is represented by a public defender is typically sentenced to a term of incarceration that is three years longer than a defendant with a private attorney. When all criminal offenses are considered, a private criminal defense attorney will typically obtain a criminal sentence that is five years shorter than a public defender.

While public defenders are exceptional attorneys, due to today's budget cuts they cannot always provide the time and attention a client needs. Private Counsel can litigate the criminal and the implied consent portion of a case and spend the time necessary to ensure the best possible outcome for a client.

DISCLAIMER:

This publication is intended to be informational only. No legal advice is being given, and no attorney-client relationship is intended to be created by reading this material. If you are facing legal issues, whether criminal or civil, seek professional legal counsel to get your questions answered.

Thomas Hagen

RosengrenKohlmeyer Law Office, Chtd

150 Saint Andrews Ct, Suite 110

Mankato, MN 56001

(507) 625-5000

Made in the USA
Monee, IL
04 November 2026

67378017R00039